C000245021

Mini Stories came about from our love of history and story-telling. Inspired by the everyday, we delve into the back stories of what surrounds us – from the wonderful natural world to innovative man-made objects we know and love. Everything comes from something and has a story.

We have gathered some of our favourites. This book is an homage to the brilliant, everyday, ordinary and extraordinary stories.

Scout Editions

SUNRISE TO SUNDOWN

The period shortly after sunrise, or before sunset during which daylight is warmer and softer, compared to when the sun is higher.

GOLDEN HOUR

Golden hour is also known as magic hour in cinematography, as it reflects the most flattering light to shoot in.

RAINBOW

A rainbow is an arch of colours visible in the sky, caused by the distribution of the sun's light by rain or other water droplets in the atmosphere. If you see a double rainbow, it's seen as very lucky!

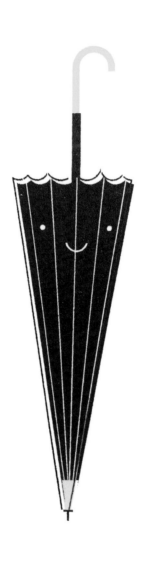

UMBRELLA

The word umbrella evolved from the Latin word 'Umbel' a flat-topped rounded flower, or umbra which means shaded/shadow. The French added 'little' in French making it umbrella. So therefore it was nicknamed 'Little Shadow'.

The Compartment Store
x Scout Editions

CLOUD

Nephology is the study of clouds. A nephophile is a person who loves clouds.

Clouds have their own names, the four core clouds: Cirro-Cumulus (Mackerel Sky), Cirrus (Mare Tails) Cumulus (Fair Weather), Cumulo-Nimbus (Thunder Clouds).

FOREST BATHING

The idea of 'forest bathing' emerged in Japan in the 1980s
as a practice called shinrin-yoku 'forest bathing' or 'taking
in the forest atmosphere'. Its aim is to inspire people
to reconnect with nature and protect the forests. It is as
simple as walking in natural environments and consciously
connecting with what's around you.

AUTUMN

Autumn marks the transition from summer to winter,
in September (Northern Hemisphere) or March (Southern
Hemisphere). One of its main features is the shedding
of leaves from deciduous trees.

TREE RINGS

The rings on a cross section of a tree can help us find out how old the tree is, and what the weather was like during each year of the tree's life. Light-coloured rings represent wood that grew in the spring and early summer, while the dark rings represent wood that grew in the late summer and autumn. As growing conditions vary each year, the rings are varied too.

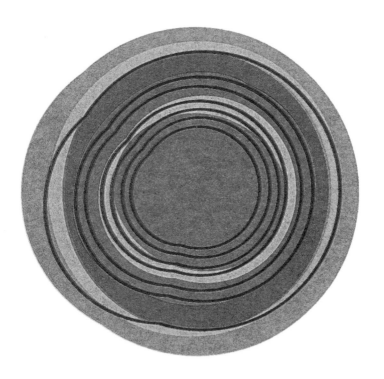

CHANGING LEAVES

As the season changes from summer to autumn and then to winter – daylight and temperature conditions also change. Leaves stop growing and the chlorophyll breaks down. The green colour from leaves fades and then turns to yellow, orange and brown tones.

ACORN

'Mighty oaks from little acorns grow'.
Great things may come from small beginnings.

GOLD LEAF

Gold leaf is gold that has been hammered into thin sheets
by gold-beating and is often used for gilding. Gold leaf
is available in a wide variety of karats and shades.
The most commonly used gold is 22-karat yellow gold.
Layering gold leaf over a surface is called gold leafing
or gilding. Traditionally used for decoration and finishes
for art and architecture.

TEEPEE

Teepees were mobile homes for nomadic tribes of the Great Plains of North America. The word tipi comes from the Lakota language. The Lakota word 'thipi' means dwelling or to dwell.

TREEHOUSE

Tree houses are usually
built for recreation, work
space, observation or as
temporary retreats.

LOG CABIN

Log cabins are made for
retreats. They were known
to be easily movable from
location to location.

HOME

'Home, Sweet Home' is a song adapted from the opera Clari, or the Maid of Milan, 1823. The lyrics were written by American actor and playwright John Howard Payne.

It is now often used as an expression of one's pleasure or relief at being in or returning home.

DALMATIAN

Dalmatians are born all-white. They're born with skin pigmentation spots, they're just obscured by their white fur. As they grow, the pigmentation shows in the fur.

HEDGEHOG

Hedgehogs are known for their prickly spines, which they have everywhere except on their face, legs and bellies. They depend on their spines for defence, both while they sleep and when they face enemies. By curling into a tight ball and tucking in their heads, tail and legs, they protect vulnerable parts of their body.

SQUIRREL

The coat of the red squirrel varies in colour with time of year and location. There are several different coat colour morphs ranging from black to red. Red coats are most common in Great Britain. The red squirrel sheds its coat twice a year, switching from a thinner summer coat to a thicker, darker winter coat.

SNOWY OWL

The Snowy Owl is from the Strigidae owl family, and is one of the largest of the owls. Their colouration is perfect for adapting to life in the north of the Arctic Circle, as they are near-perfectly camouflaged against the striking white Arctic landscapes.

BLUE TIT

A blue tit is a song bird. It is a very common sight in gardens and will visit bird feeders and tables frequently. It also has a blue cap which varies in intensity between males and females, with the male's brighter. A blue tit weighs the same as a pound coin.

BULLFINCH

The name 'bullfinch' comes from the bird's front-heavy, bull-headed appearance. The short, stubby beak is particularly adapted for feeding on buds. The bullfinch is one of the shyest garden birds, which may explain its reluctance to visit feeders.

FINCH

Finches are tiny birds, so it can be easy to overlook them. However, they are very social birds. Finches can survive up to 20 years, but most birds live from four to seven years in the wild.

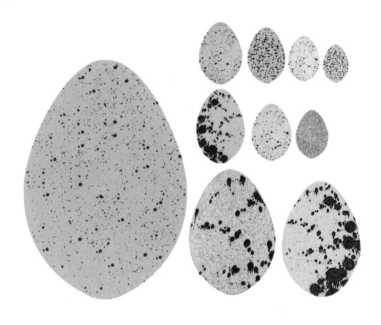

EGGS

An ostrich lays the world's largest bird's egg at an average
of 15.5cm long and 12.9cm wide, while the smallest egg laid
by any bird is that of the hummingbird at an average
of 1.2cm long and 0.5cm wide.

ROOSTER

A rooster is an adult male chicken and an adult female is called a 'hen'. Roosters are larger, usually more brightly coloured, and have larger combs on top of their heads compared to hens.

CATERPILLAR

A caterpillar has as many as 4000 muscles in its body. Using their salivary glands along the sides of their mouth, caterpillars can produce silk.

SNAIL

The term 'snail mail' was named after the snail due to its slow speed and refers to letters being carried by conventional postal delivery. It also lends its name to the 'snail trail' used to glue the envelope.

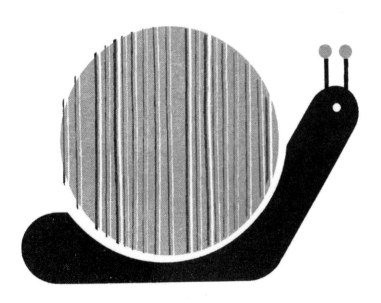

EARTHWORM

Worms can dig down over six feet underneath the surface of the soil. They can also crawl both backwards and forwards. Folk names for the earthworm include dew worm, rainworm and night crawler.

LADYBIRDS

Ladybird spots are a warning to predators. The colour
combination of black and red or orange is known as
aposematic colouration. A swarm of ladybirds is called
a 'loveliness'.

BEETLE

Beetles usually have brightly-coloured iridescent shells. This is to protect them from predators by acting as camouflage, so that they blend in with their surroundings.

The largest known beetle in the world is the titan beetle (Titanus Giganteus). It lives in the Amazon rain forests of Colombia, Ecuador, Peru, Bolivia and north Brazil. Titan beetles can grow up to 6.5 inches in length.

PIGEON

Pigeons belong to the same family as doves, the Columbidae family. There are some famous pigeons in history, from Cher Ami who carried a crucial message contained in a capsule that was attached to his leg during WWI to G.I Joe, one of the most famous pigeons in history, who helped save the British troops by delivering a very important message to them in time.

ROBIN

Robins are related to the blackbird and the nightingale, and are part of the thrush family. Both male and female robins hold their own territories in the winter, and both sing the same winter song. It is also known that the robin's favourite food is the mealworm.

HUMMINGBIRD

The hummingbird beats its wings on average 10-15 times per second. The fastest recorded rate is about 80 beats per second on an Amethyst Woodstar Hummingbird.

PEACOCK

A group of peacocks is called a party or a muster.

WOODPECKER

Woodpeckers get their name from how they forage for food. They tap on tree trunks with their strong beaks and chisel holes into the wood. There are around 180 species of woodpeckers around the world. They are part of the Picidae family.

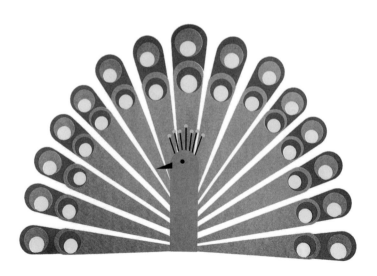

SHEEP

The term 'counting sheep' has been passed down through generations. If you can't get to sleep, 'count sheep' until you drift off. It is thought that the saying originated centuries ago when sheep herders couldn't sleep until they had counted all of their sheep to make sure none were missing.

MALLARD

Mallards are called dabbling ducks. Which means they only dip their heads under the water surface to get food. They use their bills as sensors to help determine what food is nearby.

MOUSE

Mice are keen explorers. They can squeeze through tight gaps and bite through obstacles with their strong teeth. They can also fit through a gap thats the width of a pencil.

LION

A group of lions is called a pride. They tend to live together but may spend the day in groups to hunt or share food. A pride can be made up of several generations of lionesses, a small number of breeding males and their cubs.

PENGUINS

Penguins live in groups. Within each colony, penguins remain in pairs, sometimes alone or with their offspring. A penguin's black and white colouring is called counter-shading and they are expert divers.

JELLYFISH

Many jellyfish can glow in the dark, this is especially helpful when attracting prey or distracting predators. They can also clone themselves.

SEA TURTLE

Green sea turtles feed on crabs, jellyfish and other creatures when they're young. As adults they become herbivores, mostly eating sea grasses and algae.

They can swim and reach speeds of up to 35mph. Their streamlined shell and paddle-like flippers aid their ability to swim quickly and with grace.

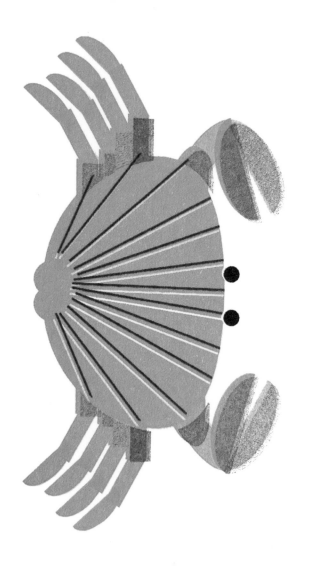

CRAB

Crabs can walk in all directions, but mostly they walk and run sideways. Crabs are decapods, meaning they have 10 legs.

SHRIMP

There are more than 2000 shrimp species. A shrimp cannot swim like a fish as it does not have fins. However it swims by quickly pulling its abdomen in toward its body. However, because of body structure, it also means that the shrimp can swim backwards.

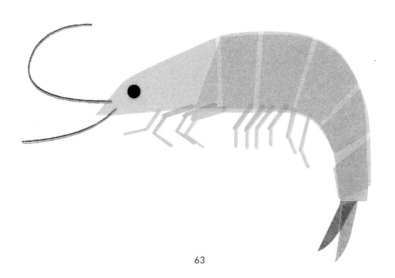

FLATFISH

A flatfish is a member of the ray-finned fish group
Pleuronectiformes. Both eyes lie on one side of the head.
Some species face their left sides upward, some face their
right sides upward, and others face either side upward.
Some well known flatfishes are plaice, dab, flounder,
dover sole, turbot and brill.

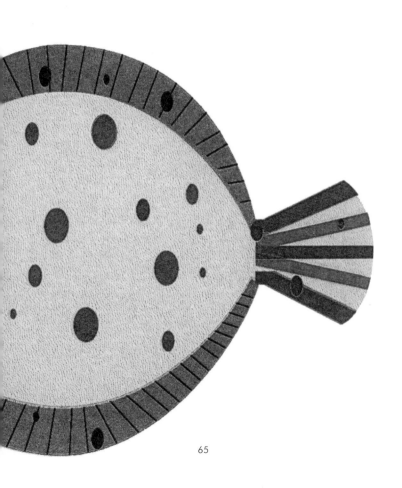

PYTHON

Pythons are one of the largest snakes. They live in the tropical areas of Africa and Asia and can be found in rainforests, savannas and deserts. Pythons swallow their prey whole, they also only eat five or six times each year.

ELEPHANTS

Elephants can cry, laugh and play. They also have incredible memories. They're social creatures, they hug by wrapping their trunks together in displays of affection.

BROWN BEAR

The brown bear is the most widely distributed bear and is found across much of northern Eurasia and North America. It is one of the largest living terrestrial members of the carnivores, rivalled in body size only by its close cousin, the polar bear.

BISON

Bison can run over 30mph, swim half a mile, and jump up to six feet in the air.

Rare Device x Scout Editions

SUNFLOWERS

Sunflowers face towards the east in the morning and west at sunset. The French word for sunflower is tournesol and the Spanish word is el girasol meaning 'to turn towards the sun'.

CHERRY BLOSSOM

Hanami means flower viewing. A popular Japanese tradition of viewing the blooming of cherry blossom in spring. Hanami parties are often held under blossom trees with family and friends to celebrate the new season.

HYDRANGEA

The name comes from the Greek 'hydor' which means water, and 'angos' meaning jar or vessel. Roughly translating as 'water barrel', referring to hydrangea's need for plenty of water.

DANDELION

The dandelion represents the three celestial bodies
of the sun, moon and stars. The yellow flower resembles
the sun, the puff ball is the moon and the dispersing seeds
resemble the stars.

It is thought that the dandelion flower opens to greet
the morning and closes in the evening to go to sleep.

SWISS CHEESE PLANT

The Swiss Cheese plant is also called Monstera Obliqua,
part of a genus of about 50 species of flowering plants
in the arum family, Araceae. The genus is named from the
Latin word for 'monstrous' and refers to the unusual leaves
with natural holes. Also known as the cheese plant as
it resembles holey cheese.

GINKGO

Ginkgo trees are dioecious, that is male and female flowers are found on separate plants. Flowering usually happens in the spring time.

BLUEBELLS

Gum from the roots of bluebells was used to glue feathers to arrows and was also used in bookbinding.

BEEHIVES

Beehives are also called hive bodies, deeps or brood boxes. This is where the bees lay their eggs and where their brood is raised. A bee can produce about one tablespoon of honey in its lifetime.

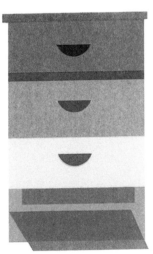

WATERING CAN

A watering can is a portable vessel with a handle and a funnel, to be used to water plants by hand. The vessel can be made of metal, ceramic or plastic.

CACTUS

The needles on cacti help protect them from animals and people. But the main function of these needles are to help shade the surface of the cactus.

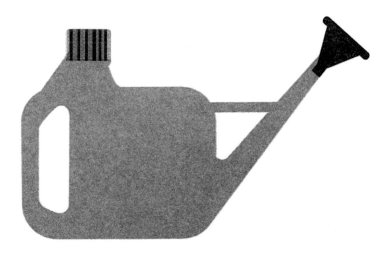

BONSAI

A bonsai-in-training is called a Potensai, the potential to be a Bonsai.

LUCKY CLOVER

The four-leaf clover is a rare variation of the common three-leaf clover. Each leaf is believed to represent something: the first is for faith, the second is for hope, the third is for love, and the fourth is for luck. It has been estimated that there are approximately 10,000 three-leaf clovers for every four-leaf clover.

88

GRAPES

Purple grapes are good for you. This is because their skin is darker in colour and they contain a higher flavonoid content. This makes them richer in antioxidants than white or green grapes.

CHERRIES

The cherry was brought to England by Henry VIII after tasting them in Belgium. The average cherry tree has 7000 cherries and can be harvested in under ten seconds with a tree shaker.

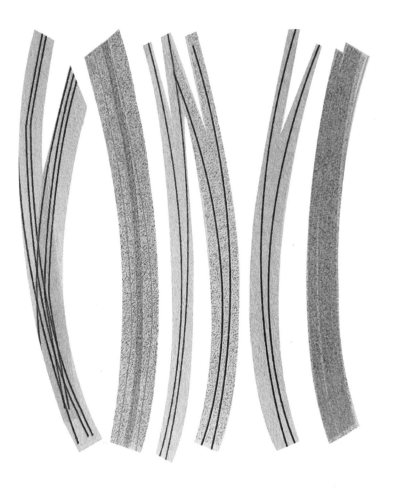

FORCED RHURBARB

Forced rhubarb is softer and sweeter than rhubarb harvested in the summer. Forcing rhubarb is a process that involves preventing light from reaching the crowns of the rhubarb plants, which triggers the production of pale stalks, perfect for cooking.

PICKLE

Pickling is the process of preserving or extending the shelf life of food, using vegetables like cucumber, beetroot, radish or peppers by fermentating them in brine or in vinegar. The process affects the food's texture and flavour, turning it into a pickle.

The word 'pickle' comes from the Dutch word 'peckel' which means pickle and brine.

COMICE PEAR

A Comice pear is the ultimate cook's pear. They have a rich taste which can be enhanced by spices. They're in season from October through to February.

According to the Pear Bureau, there are about 3000 known varieties of pears grown worldwide.

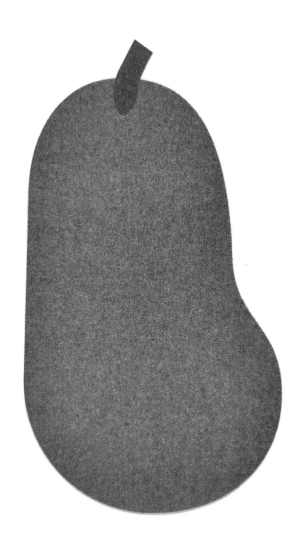

FRUIT STICKERS

The stickers found on fruits and vegetables are known
as PLU (price look-up) stickers. Each sticker contains
a price look-up number, but they're mostly branding
for the grower or farmer of the produce. A little known
fact, the stickers are edible!

Former British greengrocer Christopher Crawcour has
collected over 30,000 fruit stickers during his 25 year hobby,
one of the world's largest fruit sticker collections.

CONCORDE PEAR

Concorde pears are crunchy and sweet with a distinct vanilla flavour. They're in season from September through to December.

WATERMELON

Watermelons are both a fruit
and vegetable. Its botanical
name is Citrullus Vulgaris.
You can eat the entire fruit.
A watermelon is 92% water.
Early explorers sometimes
carried watermelons instead
of water containers.

FUJI APPLE

The Fuji apple is an apple hybrid developed by growers in Fujisaki, Japan in the late 1930s and brought to market in 1962. It originated as a cross between two American apple varieties, the Red Delicious and the Ralls Genet. Fuji apples are typically round and large.

PINEAPPLE

Pineapples first came to Europe in the 16th century, brought over by explorer Christopher Columbus.

Sailors were also known to bring them home from their travels and place them on their gateposts at home as a sign of welcome and celebration.

BANANAS

The most common bananas are the yellow bananas.
They contain a natural chemical called Serotonin which
makes you happy! They can be found in other colours,
including red, which are on the sweeter side of the banana
family. Bananas are also available in pink, purple and black.

CLEMENTINE

A clementine is a hybrid between a mandarin orange and a sweet orange. Clementine's meaning suggests peace and happiness.

SEVILLE ORANGES

The Seville orange was originally from China and was exported to the Mediterranean countries of Europe. These original orange trees were bitter in flavour, then sweet orange trees were delivered to the Portuguese coast.

These sweet oranges quickly superseded the bitter ones in this area of Spain where they are still grown. Nowadays, 15,000 tons are grown every year, mainly to make marmalade.

PUMPKIN

Pumpkins are part of the winter squash family. They are particularly popular during the autumn season when they're carved as lanterns for decoration around Halloween. Pumpkins also make great soup and pie.

MUSHROOMS

Mushrooms are fungi. There are around 14,000 species of mushrooms, from edible, medicinal to poisonous. There are also some that glow in the dark. Mushrooms have a unique umami taste too.

BENTO BOX

A bento is the Japanese take-out or home-packed meal, often for lunch. The box is organised in small compartments. Outside Japan, it is common in other East and Southeast Asian culinary styles, especially within Chinese, Korean and Singaporean cuisines, where rice is a common staple food.

SPAGHETTI

Spaghetti comes from the Italian word spago,
which translates in English to 'string' or 'twine'.

SUSHI

Sushi are small pieces of raw fish that are wrapped with rice and seaweed called nori, originating from Japan. Sushi was originally invented as a means of preservation. This was when fermented rice and salt was used to store fish to extend its shelf life, known as narezushi. The rice was thrown away and only the fish was eaten.

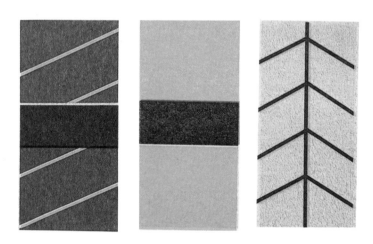

RAVIOLI

Ravioli is a type of traditional Italian pasta that is made with a filling enveloped in thin pasta dough. It is usually served with a sauce or in a broth. The word 'ravioli' derived from an Italian word avvolgere, which means 'to wrap'.

RAMEN

Ramen is the Japanese pronunciation of the Chinese lamian, meaning 'hand-pulled' noodles.

Ramen is a Japanese noodle dish. It consists of Chinese-style wheat noodles served in a meat-based broth, often flavoured with soy sauce or miso with added toppings such as sliced pork, nori and scallions. Nearly every region in Japan has its own variation of ramen, such as the tonkotsu (pork bone broth) ramen of Kyushu, and the miso ramen of Hokkaido.

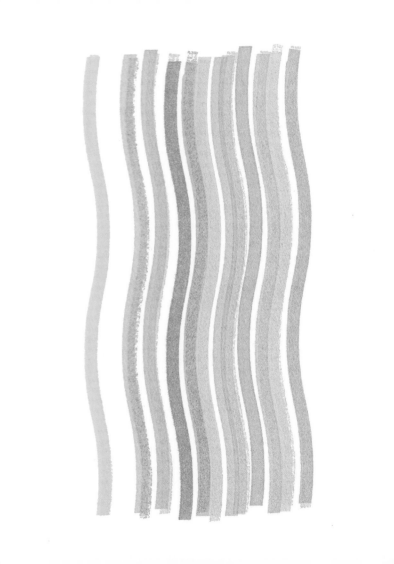

BAGUETTE

Baguettes were first created over a hundred years ago in Paris.
The name baguette translates to 'wand' or 'baton'.

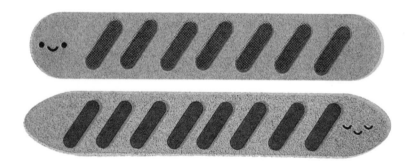

SALAMI

Salami is a cured sausage consisting of fermented and air-dried meat, usually pork. It's thought to originate in Italy from as far back as Roman times. The word salami comes from the Latin for salt – sale or to salt – salare.

OLIVE

The olive is a fruit and comes in varieties of green, purple, dark brown, black and pink colours. The only difference between green olives and black olives is ripeness, unripe olives are green, whereas fully ripe olives are black.

PEANUT

A peanut is a legume crop also known as a goober, groundnut, or monkey nut. The term 'monkey nuts' describes peanuts with the shell or pod intact.

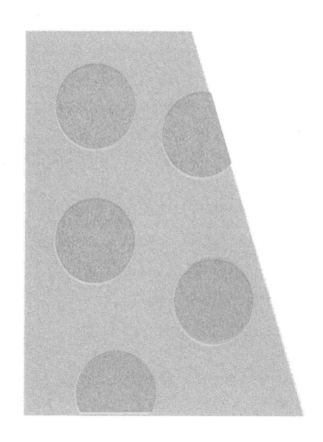

HOLEY CHEESE

Holey cheese, also known as Emmental, is a Swiss cheese
originating from the region of Emmental in Switzerland.
It is distinguished by extra large holes and its unique flavour.

CORNISH PASTY

The Cornish pasty originates from Cornwall, UK. It goes back as far as the 1200s. Mining was a thriving industry in Cornwall during that time and wives and mothers used to bake pasties for the miners. The crimped edge of a Cornish pasty was thought to have been created to be held by dirty hands of miners during their lunch break in the mines. The solid crust was often discarded after eating the rest of the pasty.

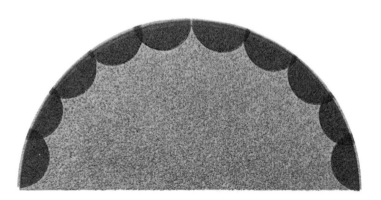

PIE BIRD

A pie bird is a hollow ceramic tool that bakers place in the centre of pies to prevent them bubbling over. They're also known as pie vents or funnels because the ceramic bird has a hollow core that allows steam to escape during baking.

CONDIMENTS

A condiment is a sauce or a relish that can be added to food to enhance its flavour or to complement it. There are numerous varieties of condiments that exists around the world in different countries, regions and cultures. The most popular condiments in the world are ketchup, mustard, soya sauce and hot sauce.

MOKA POT

The moka pot is a stove-top or electric coffee maker that brews coffee. Boiling hot water is pressurised by steam through the ground coffee. Alfonso Bialetti an Italian engineer created it in 1933 and named it after the Yemeni city of Mocha. It's an iconic piece of Italian design, known to be used by 90 percent of Italian households. It is the standard way of making coffee at home in Southern Europe.

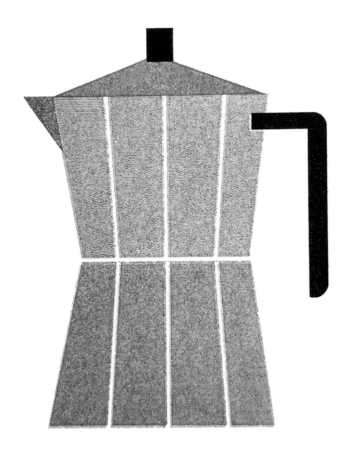

BROWN BETTY
TEAPOT

A Brown Betty is a round
teapot that is made out
of red Etruria Marl clay and
a transparent or dark brown
Rockingham glaze. Named
'Brown Betty' because of its
characteristic red clay and
brown glaze. The red clay
was discovered in Stoke-on-
Trent in Britain in 1965. This
clay resulted in a ceramic
which retained heat better.

Tea was very popular during
the Victorian era and tea
brewed in the Brown Betty
was considered of excellent
quality. This was thought to be
due to the design of the pot
which allowed the tea leaves
space to swirl around as the
water was poured into the pot
releasing more flavour.

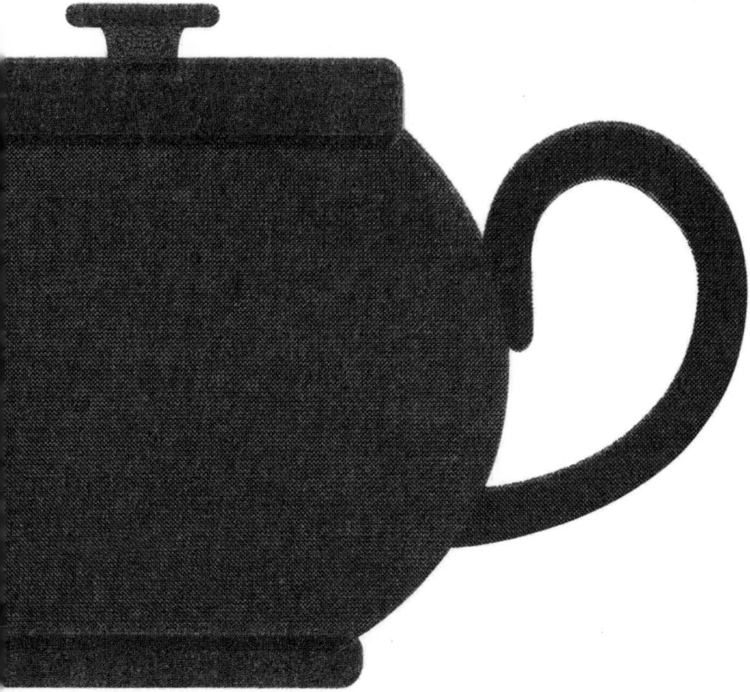

MILK BOTTLES

Milk bottles are glass bottles that store fresh milk. It was popular for milkmen to deliver each morning to peoples doorsteps. In Hampshire during the 1920s, it was noticed that blue tits learnt to peck and remove the milk top caps to access the cream on top, they were soon nicknamed the milk thieves.

FLASK

The vacuum flask is an insulating storage vessel that extends the time over which its contents remain hotter or cooler than the flask's surroundings. Invented by the British chemist and physicist Sir James Dewar in the 1890s. The vacuum flask consists of two flasks, placed one within the other and joined at the neck. Vacuum flasks are used to keep beverages hot or cold for extended time periods and are also able to keep cooked food hot longer.

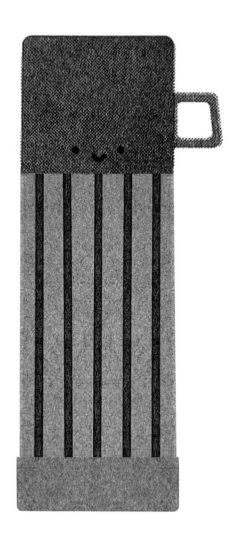

OLD-FASHIONED COCKTAIL

The Old-Fashioned cocktail acquired its name and was popularised in America but the origins of a cocktail comprising a spirit, sweetener and bitters are English and follow the creation of the first aromatic bitters by London apothecary Richard Stoughton circa 1690.

STRAWS

The first known straws were made by the Sumerians and were used for drinking beer to avoid the leftovers of fermentation that sink to the bottom.

SHOPPING BASKET

In 1936, an American businessman Sylvan Goldman and a young mechanic, Fred Young invented the first commercial shopping basket in Oklahoma, U.S. Their design had a pair of large wire baskets connected by tubular metal arms with four wheels which were known as nesting carts.

LAUNDRY BAG

The iconic red, white and blue laundry bag originated from Hong Kong, China in the 1960s and has come to represent the culture there. The nylon canvas, used to make the bags, was invented in Japan and originally used as shelter for construction sites and as protection for farmland. The bags were only made blue and white at first, then red was added to the fabric to represent luck and fortune.

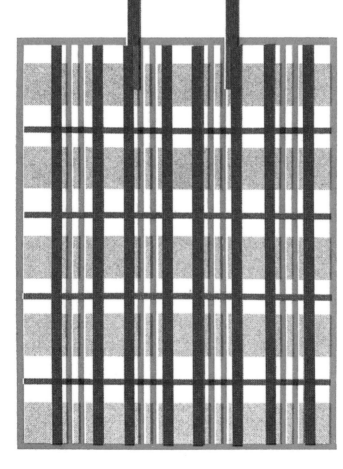

MATCHSTICKS

In 1826 a British pharmacist
named John Walker invented
the match by accident.
He was working on an
experimental paste that could
be used for guns. Whilst he
experimented, he ignited
the paste on a stick when he
scraped it against sandpaper.

PIN CUSHION

A pin cushion is a small,
stuffed cushion that is used
in sewing to store pins or
needles and to keep them tidy.

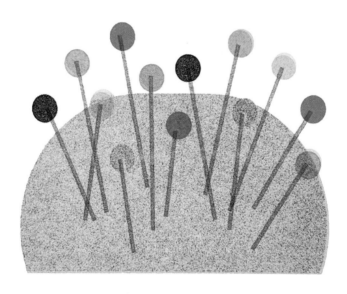

KNITTING NEEDLES

A knitting needle or knitting pin is a tool in hand-knitting to produce knitted fabrics. They are long and tapered at the end. The largest knitting needles made measure 446cm long with a diameter of 9cm. They were made by Elizabeth Bond from the UK.

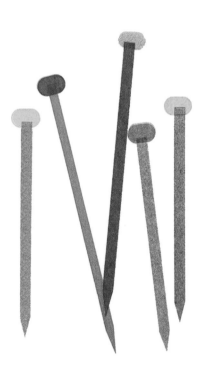

SEWING MACHINE

Englishman Thomas Saint designed the first sewing machine of its kind which was hand-powered. Isaac Singer in the U.S. is credited with the first sewing machine in 1851. In 1889, the electric sewing machine for use in the home was designed and marketed by Singer. Singer has been the world famous brand of sewing machines for decades.

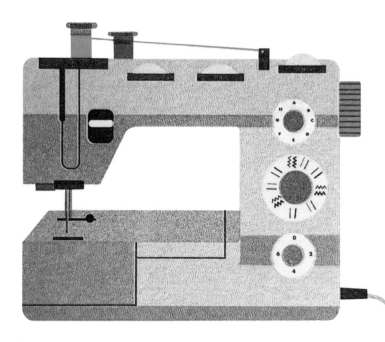

HAIR DRYER

In 1890 the first hair dryer
was invented by French stylist
Alexander Godefroy. His
invention was a large, seated
version that consisted of a
bonnet that attached to the
chimney pipe of a gas stove.
Godefroy invented it for use
in his hair salon in France,
and it was not portable
or hand-held. The hand-held,
household hair dryer first
appeared in 1920.

SPECTACLES

Glasses became common in the 1660s, as a pair of lenses
set in a frame and used to wear on the nose and ears to help
correct or assist eyesight. The word spectacles was adopted
in the 18th century and comes from the Latin 'spectare',
to observe or to look at. Other words used: blinkers,
eyeglasses, prisms, bifocals, specs, sunglasses, jiggers,
field-glasses, opera-glasses and nose glasses.

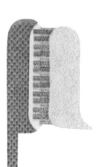

TOOTHBRUSH

From 3000 B.C.,
the ancient Egyptians
constructed toothbrushes
from twigs and leaves
to clean their teeth.

The first mass-produced
toothbrush was made
by William Addis of
Clerkenwald, England
around 1780.

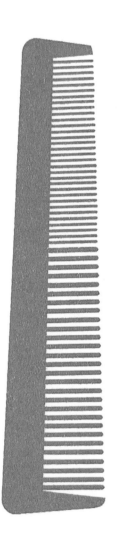

COMB

A comb is a tool that consists of a row of thin teeth that is pulled through the hair to untangle and style.

Combs have been used since prehistoric times, discovered dating back 5000 years ago in Persia.

SOCKS

In ancient times, socks were made from leather or matted animal hair. In the late 16th century, machine-knit socks were first produced. In the 1800s both man-made and machine-knit socks were manufactured. Machine-knitted socks became more popular in the 19th century.

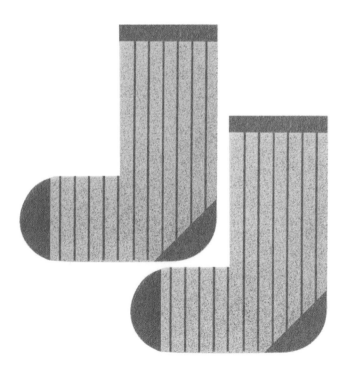

BROGUES

The brogue derives from the Gaeilge bróg (Irish), and the Gaelic bròg (Scottish) for 'shoe'. It is a style of low-heeled shoe or boot traditionally characterised by multiple-piece, sturdy leather uppers with decorative perforations.

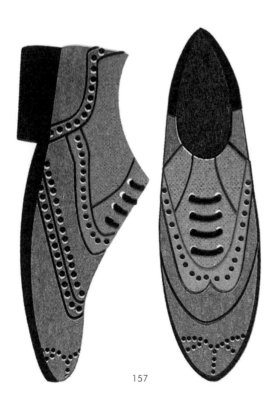

BOBBY PINS

In the 1920s during the flapper era, Luis Marcus a cosmetics manufacturer from San Francisco designed the bobby pin. It was created to hold in place the bobbed-length wavy hair that was part of the flapper trend at the time. Marcus thought about naming the pin after himself, but then decided to name it bobby after the bobbed hairstyle.

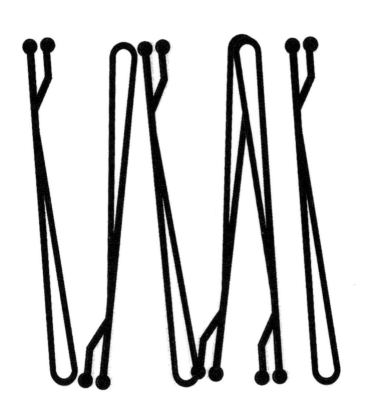

ROLLERSKATE

Roller-skating was invented
in 1735 by John Joseph Merlin,
a Belgian who famously
introduced his new wheeled
shoes at a party in London.
Monsieur Petitbled patented
the roller-skate in 1819.

SHUTTLECOCK

Shuttlecocks were traditionally
made from feathers that
were gathered from the wing
of a goose. It takes about
16 feathers to make the
shuttlecock. They were also
known as a 'bird' or 'birdie'.

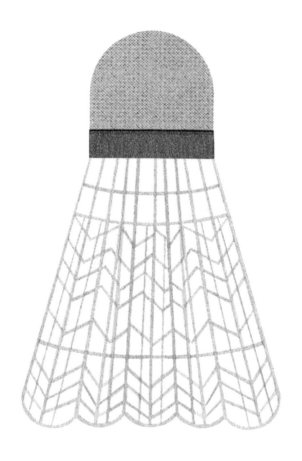

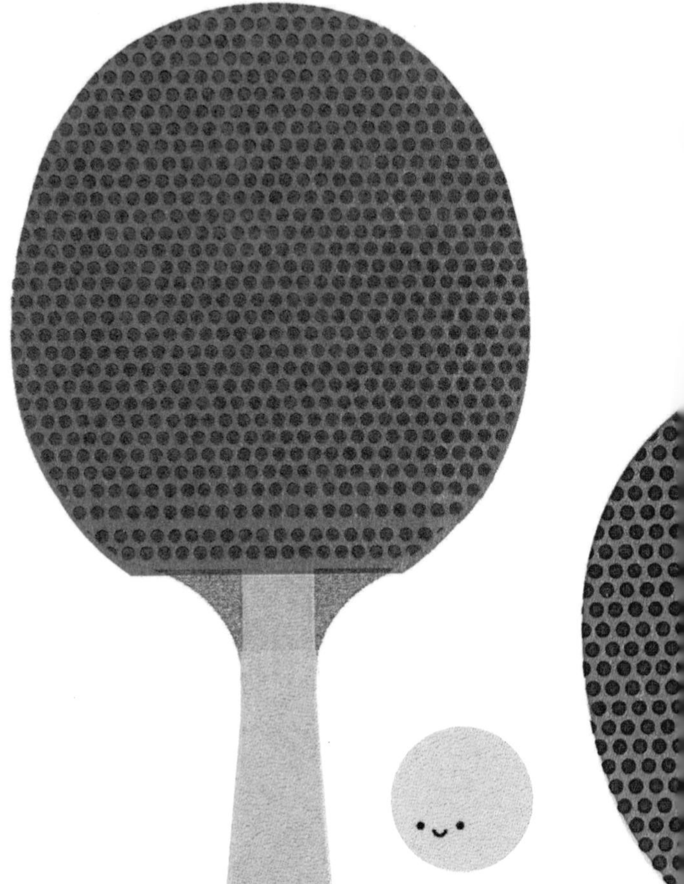

PING-PONG

Table tennis is also known as ping-pong. It is a sport in which two or four players hit a lightweight ball back and forth across a table using small bats. It derived from 'ping pang qiu' in Mandarin Chinese (same pronunciation) which translates literally to 'ping pong ball'.

The sport originated in Victorian England, where it was played among the upper-class as an after-dinner game. It's thought that makeshift versions of the game were developed by British military officers in India around the 1860s who brought it back with them.

TENNIS COURT

There are four main types
of surface for tennis courts:
grass, clay, hard and artificial
grass. The deep red coloured
clay courts are considered the
slowest surface as they slow
down the speed of the ball. The
grass surface is the fastest of all
the surfaces due to its slippery
surface. The ball has a lower
bounce as the soil is softer.

FOOTBALL PITCH

The playing surface for the
game of football is made up
of dimensions and markings,
defined by 'The Field of Play'.
The pitch is usually made
of natural or artificial turf.

CHESS

Chess is one of the world's most popular games, played by millions of people worldwide. The longest chess game is 269 moves between Ivan Nikolic vs. Goran Arsovic, Belgrade, 1989. The game ended in a draw. The game lasted over 20 hours. The shortest game ever recorded between two grand masters, was in four moves. Lazard defeated Gibaud in a chess café in Paris in 1924.

KIMONO

A kimono is a traditional Japanese garment and the national dress of Japan. It is usually worn with an obi belt, alongside other accessories, such as zori shoes and tabi socks.

AFRICAN MASKS

Masks serve an important role in rituals or ceremonies for various purposes like ensuring a good harvest, addressing tribal needs in times of peace or conveying spiritual rituals and traditional ceremonies.

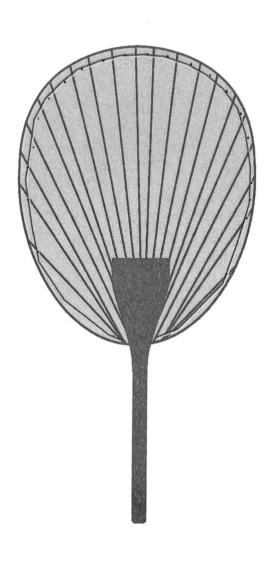

PAPER FAN

Traditional Japanese fans are made from paper and bamboo, usually with a design painted on them. Non-folding fans, called Uchiwa, are popular as part of seasonal traditions and are often given as gifts during these times.

XYLOPHONE

The xylophone is a member of the percussion family of instruments. The name comes from two Greek words: xylon, meaning 'wood' and phone, meaning 'voice'.

Xylophone bars are created with different lengths, which produce different sounds. Shorter xylophone bars produce higher notes and the longer bars produce lower notes.

TRUMPET

The English word 'trumpet' was first used in the late
14th century. The word came from old French 'trompette'
which is a diminutive of trompe. The word 'trump' meaning
'trumpet' was first used in English in 1300.

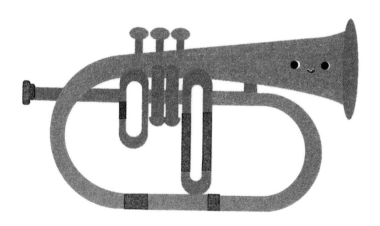

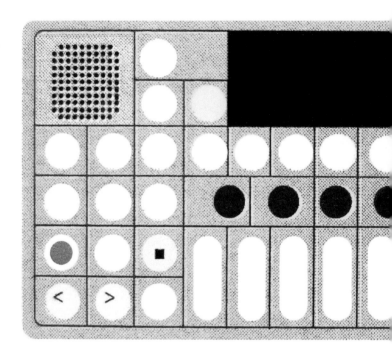

SYNTHESIZER

A synthesizer is an electronic instrument that uses digital or analog processes to create, sample and produce audible sounds.

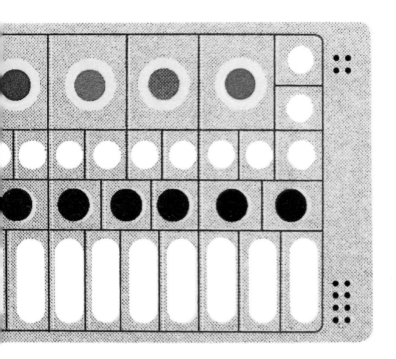

175

RECORD PLAYER

A record player was also known as a phonograph and a gramophone. It has been called a record player since the 1940s, and more recently a turntable. The record player is a device for analogue recording and the reproduction of sound.

RADIO

Italian inventor Guglielmo Marconi first developed the idea of a radio, or wireless telegraph, in the 1890s. In 1893, Nikolai Tesla, another well known inventor, demonstrated the first wireless radio in St Louis, Missouri. There are many controversies around the invention of the radio. Most people agree that either Nikolai Tesla or Guglielmo Marconi were responsible for the first radio invented.

Nikolai Tesla filed patents for his radio, which were granted in 1900. However, Marconi was the first person to transmit radio signals across the Atlantic Ocean.

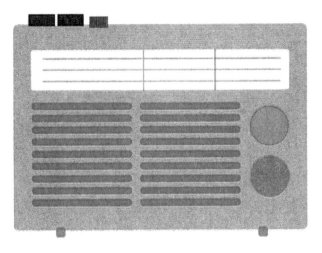
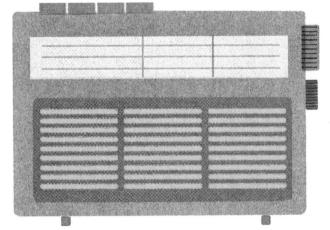

RISO

In Japanese 'Riso' means 'ideal'. Riso is also known as
risograph, a brand of digital stencil duplicators from Japan.
It was first released in Japan in 1986. They were initially used
for high-volume printing. Similar to screen-printing, artwork
is scanned from its original and is burnt onto a wax master.
The master is then fed through a print drum, layer by layer
to print each separate coloured layer.

Riso-printing is an eco-friendly, energy efficient print process
with no harmful emissions and minimal waste. It also prints
with soy-based inks.

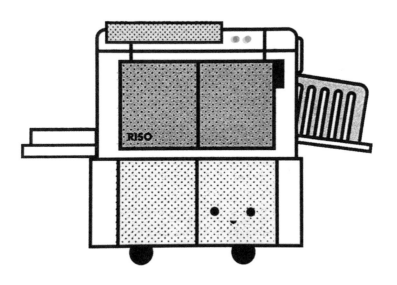

ANGLEPOISE LAMP

A car designer called George Carwardine designed the
Anglepoise lamp in his garden shed in 1932. It was originally
intended to be part of a vehicle suspension system but
he realised that it would make the perfect lamp as it
could be positioned at any angle with the lightest touch.
The mechanics of the iconic lamp have remained largely
unchanged for 90 years.

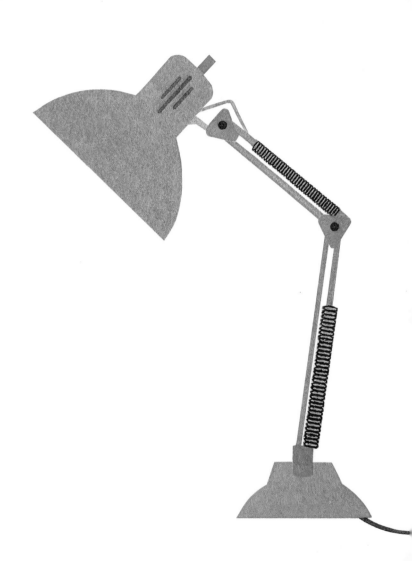

ROBOT

The earliest robots were created in the early 1950s by George C. Devol, an inventor from Louisville, Kentucky. The largest robot known to be created is robot Mononofu. At 8.5 metres tall, it weighs over seven tons. It was built by Japanese engineer Masaaki Nagumo.

PORCELAIN

Porcelain production began for the first time in Japan in 1616 in the region of Arita, located in Saga Prefecture on the island if Kyushu. Arita is home to highly specialised craftspeople that are continuously looking for new ways to preserve and advance the town's unique artisan culture.

Made By Kihara x Scout Editions

KOKESHI

Handmade out of wood, with a simple trunk and enlarged head, Kokeshi dolls originate from northern Japan. They're thought to date back to the early 19th century, when woodworkers began using their skills to make simple dolls to sell as toys or souvenirs.

NUTCRACKER

Nutcrackers in the form of wood carvings of a soldier, knight or king have existed since the 15th century. Figurative nutcrackers are a good luck symbol in Germany. A folk tale recounts that a puppet-maker won a nut-cracking challenge by creating a doll with a mouth for cracking the nuts.

RUDOLPH

Rudolph the Red-Nosed Reindeer is a legendary reindeer. A young fawn, who barely has antlers, with a glowing red nose. He's known as Santa's ninth reindeer, the lead reindeer helping Santa pull his sleigh. His nose is so bright that it illuminates their way through the snow at night.

GINGERBREAD HOUSE

The biggest gingerbread house ever made measured 20ft tall in Texas, Tennessee. Made with 1800lbs of butter, 7200 eggs, 7200lbs of flour and 3000lbs of brown sugar. And with massive amounts of sweets.

CHRISTMAS TREE

Christmas trees are evergreen trees, usually a fir, pine or spruce tree. It is believed that decorating Christmas trees originated in 16th century Germany. They were first decorated with food such as apples, nuts and dates.

SNOWMAN

Austria is home to the
world's tallest snowman.
The snowman, nicknamed
'Riesi' which roughly
translates to 'giant'
in English, measures
a gigantic 38.04 metres.

IGLOO

An igloo is also known
as an iglu, from the Inuit
word for 'house' or
'shelter'. It was traditionally
associated with Inuits.
When they went on their
hunting trips they built a
temporary house to protect
themselves from the cold.

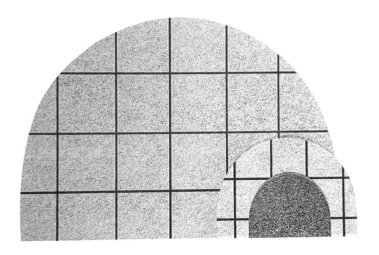

SNOW GLOBE

Erwin Perzy from Austria invented the snow globe in 1900 by accident, when he was trying to improve the brightness of an electric light bulb. It is now a family business. His grandson Erwin Perzy III continued with his grandfather's legacy.

SANTA CLAUS

Saint Nicholas, also known as Santa Claus, was born in 270 AD, so he would now be 1749 years old. Santa's sleigh is led by his reindeer: Dasher, Dancer, Prancer, Vixen, Comet, Cupid, Dunder, Blixem and Rudolph.

CHRISTMAS PUDDING

The first version of the pudding originated in the 14th century. The British made porridge called 'frumenty', made of beef and mutton with raisins, wine, currants and spices. The pudding tended to be more like soup and was eaten during the festive season.

CAKE

It is believed that the first birthday cake was made in Germany in the Middle Ages. Cakes originally were bread-like and later became a much sweeter version, called Geburtstagskuchen.

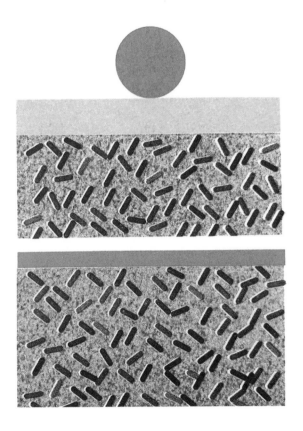

CHOCOLATE

Chocolate was created in Mexico over 4000 years ago.
It's there that the first cacao plants were found and they
were first to turn the cacao plant into chocolate.

There are different grades of chocolate. It varies in taste,
usually the higher the percentage of cacao, the more intense
the chocolate flavour or more bitter or sweet it tastes.

TAIYAKI

Taiyaki is a Japanese fish-shaped cake. It imitates the shape of the Tai (a Japanese sea bream), which it's named after. The most common filling may be custard, chocolate, cheese or sweet potato.

JELLY

Jelly is made with a sweetened and flavoured gelatin.
This kind of dessert was first recorded as jelly by Hannah
Glasse in her 18th-century book The Art of Cookery,
appearing in a layer of trifle.

ICE CREAM

Ice cream cones were invented during the 1904 World's Fair in St. Louis, Missouri. This was when large demands forced an ice cream vendor to find help from a nearby waffle vendor. Together they made history.

POPSICLES

The first Popsicle ice pop was created in 1905 by an 11-year-old named Frank Epperson in the U.S. He invented it by accident, after playing outside all day. The next day he found he had left a cup of soda with the stirring stick still in it out in the garden, it had frozen overnight.

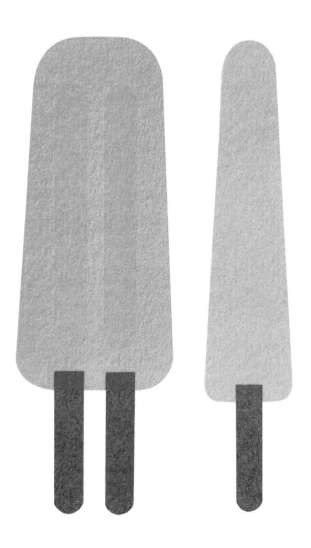

CANDY FLOSS

In 1897 a dentist called William Morrison and a confectioner John Wharton created candy floss in Nashville, Tennessee. They launched cotton candy in 1908 at the World's Fair.

The English call it candy floss because the spun sugar was reminiscent of 'floss', an embroidery thread, similar to cotton. The Americans call it cotton candy, and the French – barbe papa, which means – daddy's beard!

DOUGHNUT

To fully cook the insides of a doughnut, the dough would have to stay in the oil for too long a time, which would lead to the outsides becoming burnt. Punching a hole in the middle of the dough allows the insides and the outsides to cook evenly, creating a perfect doughnut.

PRETZEL

Pretzels first originated in Germany and the pronunciation in German is Brezel. Pretzels are a type of baked bread made from dough that is commonly shaped into a knot. The traditional pretzel shape is a distinctive symmetrical form, with the ends of a long strip of dough intertwined and then twisted back onto itself like a bow.

WAGASHI

Wagashi are traditional Japanese confectionery that are often served with green tea. Wagashi are usually made from plant-based ingredients, filled with mocha, anko (azuki bean paste) and fruit.

BON BON

Christmas crackers were invented in 1846 by British confectioner, Thomas Smith. On a trip to Paris he found a bon-bon, a sugar almond wrapped in tissue paper. He decided to take this idea and included poems wrapped around the sweet. He then developed it further by adding the cracking noise when it's pulled apart.

In later years he decided to add a surprise gift and a party hat. Eventually the poems were replaced by novelty jokes.

KIOSK

A kiosk is a small cubicle or open-fronted booth where goods and services are sold, such as refreshments, tickets and newspapers through an open window.

VENDING MACHINE

Japan has the highest density of vending machines worldwide, they are called jidōhanbaik. Vending machines can be found all over cities, towns and also the countryside selling tobacco, drinks, books, clothing, toys, food, confectionery to umbrellas.

The first vending machine in Japan dispensed tobacco and was made by Tawaraya Koshichi, a furniture designer and inventor in 1888. It wasn't until the late 1950s when vending machines became popular and in the everyday life of Japanese culture.

DECK CHAIR

A deckchair is a portable folding chair with a single strip of fabric as the backrest and seat. It is used for leisure, originally on the deck of an ocean liner or cruise ship.

John Thomas Moore took out a patent for adjustable folding chairs in 1886 and manufactured them in Macclesfield from 1887. Nowadays deck chairs are popular on beaches.

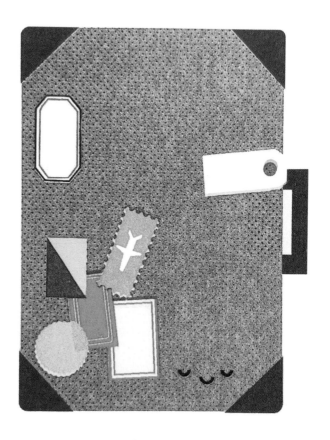

SUITCASE

A suitcase is a form of luggage. It is often a flat, rectangular-shaped bag with rounded square corners. Vinyl, leather or cloth suitcases may have a metal frame. Hardshell suitcases open on hinges like a door.

Other words for suitcase: baggage, gear, belongings, kit, goods, paraphernalia, accoutrements, bags, cases and trunks.

SAILBOAT

Portuguese explorer Ferdinand Magellan was known to have master-minded the first expedition to sail around the world from 1519 to 1522.

On average it can take between three to five years to sail around the world. However, the fastest time to do this is 42 days by French skipper, Francois Gabart in 2017.

HELICOPTER

Helicopters can get to people in hard-to-reach places, such as mountains and oceans because of their size and mobility. Their ability to hover and land without a runway, means that it can also get to places much quicker and they're ideal for moving large objects.

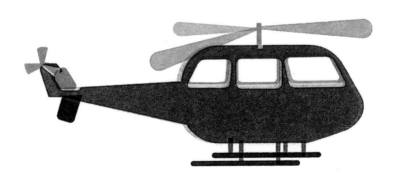

HOUSEBOAT

A houseboat is a boat that has been designed or modified to be used primarily as a home. Some houseboats are not motorised, because they are usually moored, kept stationary at a fixed point and often tethered to land to provide utilities.

HOT AIR BALLOON

The longest distance travelled in a hot air balloon was by Bertrand Piccard and Brian Jones. They flew a hot air balloon – the Breitling Orbiter 3 around the world, covering 46,759 km (29,055 mi) in 19 days, 21 hours and 55 minutes.

BICYCLE

The bicycle has had many names over the years from 'velocipede', 'hobby horse', 'draisine', 'running machine' and now the bicycle. There are over one billion bicycles being used all around the world at present.

LONDON UNDERGROUND

The London Underground first opened in 1863 with six stations and is also known as the Tube. There are no obvious reasons why each line is the colour they are, but the oldest lines are the primary colours and it may be a coincidence that London's greener areas are on the district line, which is a green line, which also happens to have the word 'green' in many of the place names.

BAKERLOO LINE

CENTRAL LINE

CIRCLE LINE

DISTRICT LINE

HAMMERSMITH & CITY LINE

METROPOLITAN LINE

NORTHERN LINE

PICCADILLY LINE

VICTORIA LINE

ELIZABETH LINE

WATERLOO & CITY LINE

COLLAGE

The word collage is from the French word 'coller' which means to paste or to glue. It is a technique used in art, primarily in the visual arts, where the artwork is made from an assemblage of different forms, to create a whole or finished piece.

BAUHAUS

The Bauhaus movement was founded in 1919 by German architect Walter Gropius.

A school of ideas, experimenting in applied arts, design, architecture and educational methods, it was famous for the approach to design that it publicised and taught.

The German term Bauhaus means 'building house' also known as 'School of Building'.

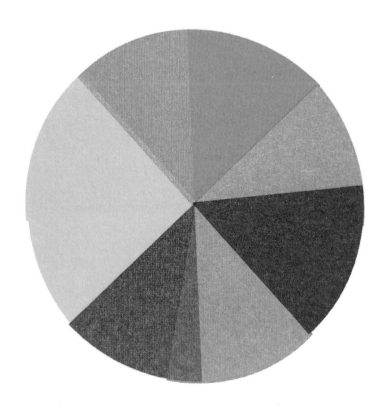

COLOUR WHEEL

The word colour derives
from the Latin word 'colos'
which means 'a cover'.
Analogous colours are
groups of three colours
that sit next to each other
on the colour wheel, sharing
a common colour with one
being the dominant colour
which tends to be a primary
or secondary colour and
a tertiary.

COLOUR BLOCKING

Colour-blocking is an
exploration of colours.
Usually pairing two or more
colours together to make
interesting and complem-
entary combinations.

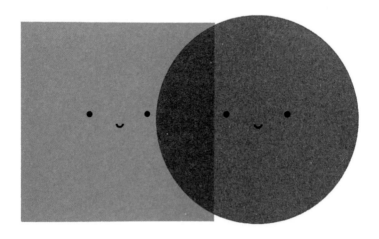

ERASERS

'Anyone who has never made a mistake has never tried anything new'

Albert Einstein

Present & Correct x Scout Editions

STATIONERY

'There was something very comfortable in having plenty of stationery'

Charles Dickens

Present & Correct x Scout Editions

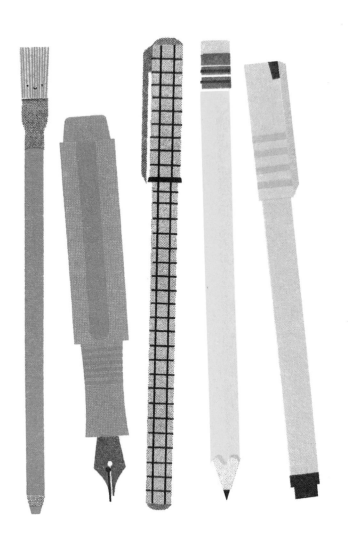

BOOK

A bookworm is a person who loves reading. Another meaning is when the larva of a wood-boring beetle feeds on the paper and glue in books.

PENCIL

'Success is a worn down pencil'

Robert Rauschenberg

CRAYONS

The word 'crayon' dates back to the 16th century, from the French word for chalk that is 'craie' and 'ola' from the word oleaginous, which means oily.

Crayola is an American manufacturing company specialising in art supplies. It is best known for its crayons. The name 'Crayola' was given by Alice Binney, wife, former school teacher and co-founder of Crayola along with her husband Edwin Binney and cousin Joseph Binney in New York. The first box of Crayola crayons was produced in 1903 as an eight piece box that contained orange, yellow, green, blue, violet, brown and black crayons.

JAPANESE BRUSHES

Japanese paint and ink brushes are well known for their quality and craftsmanship. The fude brush is a popular ink brush that is used in many traditional crafts such as calligraphy, ink painting, pottery and lacquer ware. The hira-fude, which is a flat brush is the most popular brush for painting flat and large surfaces.

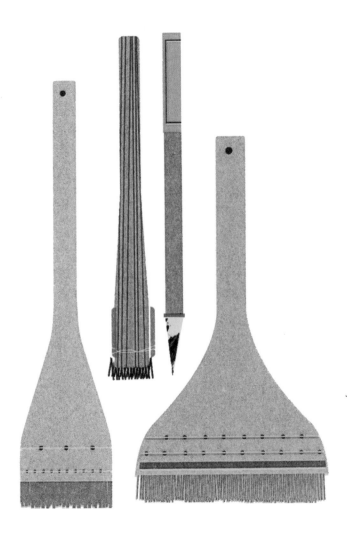

SECURITY PATTERNS

A security envelope is an envelope that has a pattern printed on the inside so that when it is held up towards light, the contents of the envelope cannot be seen, providing a protective barrier. The envelope and inside pattern can be any colour or style, but the most common are white or brown envelopes with a blue or black pattern inside.

PAR AVION

EPHEMERA

'Great things are done
by a series of small things
brought together'

Vincent Van Gogh

Present & Correct x Scout Editions

AIR MAIL ENVELOPE

'More than kisses, letters
mingle souls'

John Donne

AIR MAIL
PAR AVION

PAPER CLIPS

It's not known exactly who invented the paper clip or where it was invented. There have been various designs and variations of the paper clip from 1896 to the 1950s.
The first patent for paper clips wasn't actually for the clips but for the machines that would make them. In 1899, William Middlebrook received a patent for a machine that would make a paper clip. He called it the Gem Clip and it looked very similar to the clips we use today.

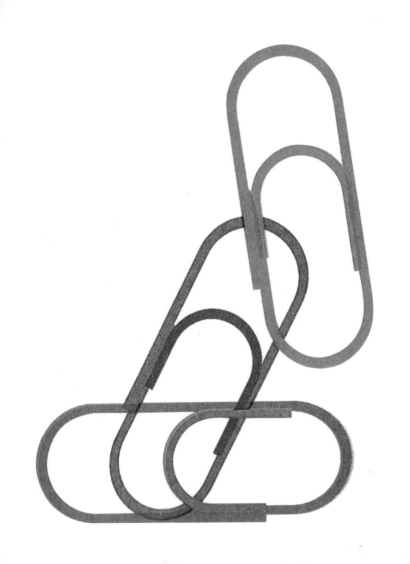

POSTAGE STAMP

The Penny Black was the world's first adhesive postage stamp used in a public postal system. It was first issued in the UK on 1 May 1840. The stamp features a profile of Queen Victoria.

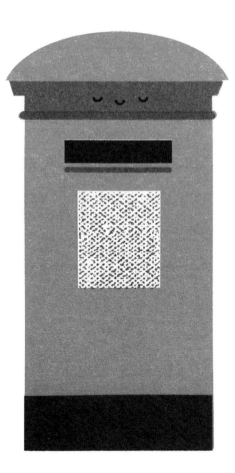

POST BOX

Many of the UK's early post boxes were painted green to blend in with the landscape in the countryside. Later they were repainted the iconic 'pillar box red' to make them more visible.

OLIVETTI VALENTINE TYPEWRITER

In the original 1960s user guide for the Valentine typewriter, it reads "Dear Valentine, this is to tell you that you are my friend as well as my Valentine, and that I intend to write you lots of letters".

OLIVETTI LETTERA 32 TYPEWRITER

Designed by Marcello Nizzoli, Italy 1963.

Before Breakfast x Scout Editions

APPLE MAC COMPUTER

The first Macintosh computer was launched in 1984 by Steve Jobs. It was called the Macintosh 128K, originally released as the Apple Macintosh, the original Apple personal computer.

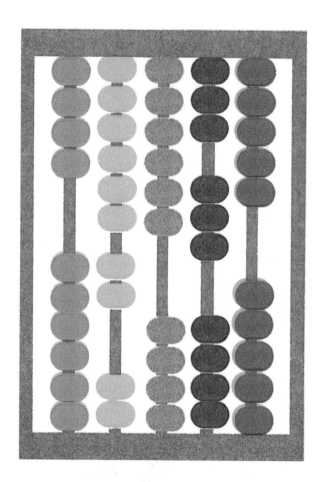

ABACUS

The abacus is a counting frame and tool which has been used for many centuries. It was first used in the ancient Far East, Europe, China and Russia. The word abacus derived from the Greek word 'abax' which means 'tabular form'. It was thought to be invented in ancient Babylon between 300 and 500 BC. The abacus was the first counting machine, before which people were using their fingers, stones or other types of natural materials or objects to help count.

CALCULATOR

The first electronic calculator was created in the early 1960s and the pocket-sized devices became available in the 1970s.

Present & Correct x Scout Editions

275

POLAROID CAMERA

The Polaroid camera was invented by Edwin Land in 1948, in Boston, Massachusetts, U.S. The term, 'polaroid' comes from one of the ingredients used to make instant photos. Polaroid is a plastic sheet with special chemicals on the top layer.

The camera and the film went on sale in 1948 at a department store in Boston and the camera sold out in minutes. There are many variations and styles of the Polaroid camera today.

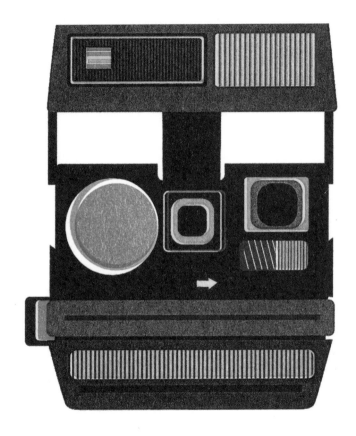

CAMERA

Joseph E. Davies, an American lawyer and diplomat who served under Franklin D. Roosevelt, suggested while having his picture taken in 1943, that the formula to taking a good picture was saying 'cheese', as it creates an automatic smile.

The Photographers Gallery x Scout Editions

CINE CAMERA

Cine Super 8mm film cameras were first manufactured in 1965 by Kodak for their newly introduced amateur film format, which replaced the Standard 8mm film format. Manufacturing continued until the rise in popularity of video cameras in the mid 1970s. Super 8 cameras made shooting films easier and more affordable. They were also portable and fun to use.

FILM ROLL

The blue hour arrives shortly before sunrise and after sunset, when the sun's horizon is just below the horizon. This is when the atmosphere has a deep indigo colour. During the blue hour, using a slower shutter speed when taking photos will help ensure photos are exposed better.

The Photographers Gallery x Scout Editions

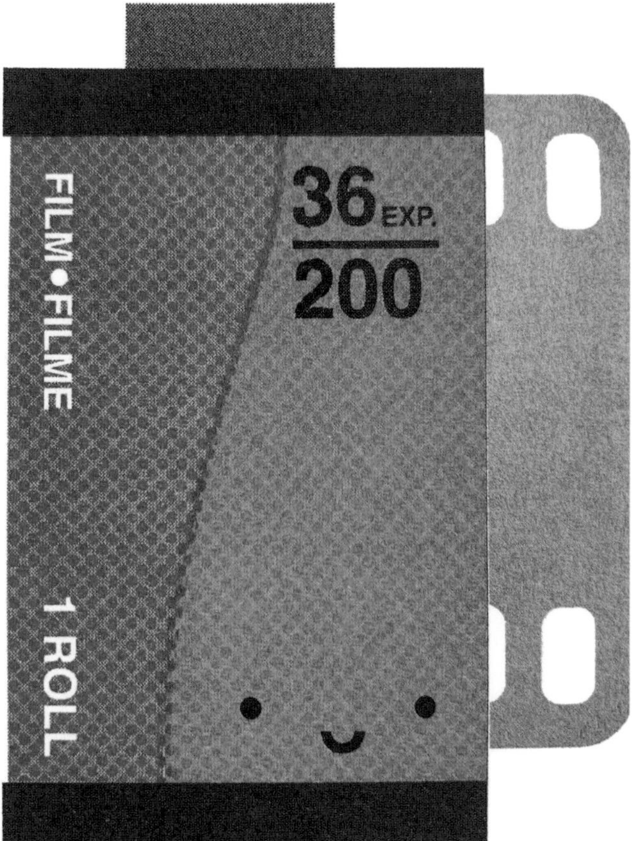
FILM • FILME
1 ROLL
36 EXP.
200

BINOCULARS

Binoculars are also known as field glasses. They are two refracting telescopes mounted side-by-side, allowing the viewer to use both eyes when viewing distant objects. The noun comes from an adjective, binocular, which means 'having two eyes', or 'involving both eyes', from the Latin word bina which means 'two by two', 'in pairs' and 'double'.

ASTRONAUT

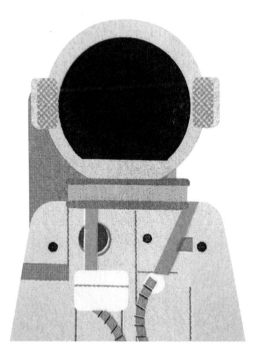

On 21 July 1969, American astronaut Neil Armstrong became the first person to walk on the Moon. He stepped out of the Apollo 11 lunar module and onto the Moon's surface and said, 'That's one small step for man, one giant leap for mankind'.

THE PLANETS

Some scientists believe that around a billion years ago
Neptune and Uranus may have switched their places
in the solar system.

'TO THE MOON AND BACK'

A phrase or notion using the distance from the Earth
to the Moon and the return trip (455,000 miles or so)
as a measure or to express a quantum of love as
a measurement of distance.

MINI STORIES

The illustrations in this book were originally riso-printed. They have been scanned from the riso prints therefore may have imperfections and offsetting may have occurred. This is part of the riso print process.

SCOUT EDITIONS
scouteditions.co.uk

Copyright on projects and their related imagery is held by Scout Editions.

COUNTER-PRINT
counter-print.co.uk

© 2023 Counter-Print

British Library cataloguing-in-publication data: A catalogue of this book can be found in the British Library.

ISBN: 978-1-915392-01-5

First published in the United Kingdom in 2023 by Counter-Print.

Edited and produced by Counter-Print and Scout Editions.
Designed by Counter-Print and Scout Editions.
Printing and Binding by 1010 Printing International Limited Printed in China.